Thank You, Thank You, Thank You, God

Christine Harder Tangvald
Illustrated by Terry Boles

Dedicated with love to Kjerste René Tangvald.
I am SO THANKFUL . . . for YOU!

Chariot Books™ is an imprint of David C. Cook Publishing Co.
David C. Cook Publishing Co., Elgin, Illinois 60120
David C. Cook Publishing Co., Weston, Ontario
Nova Distribution, Newton Abbot, England
THANK YOU, THANK YOU, THANK YOU, GOD
© 1993 by Christine Harder Tangvald for text and Terry Boles for illustrations.
Cover and interior design by Jeffrey P. Barnes
First Printing, 1993. Printed in the United States of America
97 96 95 94 93   5 4 3 2 1
ISBN 0-7814-0007-4 LC 92-70359

Chariot Books™
David C. Cook Publishing Co.

Thank You

HELLO TIME

Well, hello!
My name is Christine, and I'm **so glad** to meet you.

What is your name?
My, what a wonderful name you have. And I'll bet **you** are wonderful, too!

Would you like to have some FUN with me? You **would**? Oh, **GOOD**!
I want to have some fun with you, too—going through this book of FUN-TO-DO devotions.

Do you ever say THANK YOU?
I'll bet you do, because saying THANK YOU is an important thing to do, isn't it?
We say THANK YOU for all kinds of things—
When we get a birthday present, we say THANK YOU!
When someone takes us on a merry-go-round ride, we say THANK YOU!
When someone pushes us on a swing—high, high, HIGHER—Whee!
then we say THANK YOU! THANK YOU **VERY** MUCH!

Yes, saying THANK YOU **is** important.

One of God's wonderful Bible verses even says so. It says,

VERSE TIME

"In everything give thanks . . . "
(I Thessalonians 5:18a)

and WE DO!

You see, God likes it when we tell Him THANK YOU. He likes it a lot!
If you could say THANK YOU to God right now for something, what would

Write it here

Is it hard to think of something? Well, if you go through this book with me,
we will find a hundred, billion, TRILLION things to say THANK YOU for.
And not only that! We are going to make a terrific, huge, long THANK-YOU CHAIN just for **FUN**!
I'm excited. I hope you are, too! Here we go. . . .

One thing we can tell God THANK YOU for is our **VERY OWN SELF**!

God gave me two blue EYES!
How many eyes
do **you** have?_____

What color are they?

_____

Thank You, God, for EYES!

God gave me two nice
EARS! How many ears do
you have?_____

What is your favorite thing
to listen to?

_____

Thank You, God, for EARS!

How many teeth do you
have? _____

Show them to me. Wow!
That **is** a lot of teeth!
Thank You, God,
for TEETH!

3

How many FINGERS do you have?_____   How many TOES?_____

How many fingers **plus** toes?

_____ + _____ = _____ !
  fingers   toes

Thank You, God, for FINGERS and TOES!

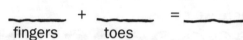

How many HAIRS do you think you have on the top of your head?
(I hope you didn't try to COUNT all of them. That would take all day!)

But, GUESS WHAT! God knows how many hairs
you have on your head!
He knows because He **made** you!
And He did a **very** good job, didn't He?

You see, God made you **exactly** the way
He wants you to be, and I'm GLAD because,

I think you are GREAT!
I think you are NEAT!
I think you are NICE!
from your head to your FEET!

4

PRAYER TIME

Oh, yes,
THANK YOU, THANK YOU, THANK YOU, GOD,
for making ME SO SPECIAL!
Amen

GOOD-BYE TIME

Boy, saying THANK YOU can be fun. I can hardly wait until next time to find out more exciting things to be thankful for . . . about YOU! See you then! Good-bye!

SOMETHING FUN-TO-DO

Let's make a huge, long, long THANK-YOU CHAIN. Let's see how **long** we can make it by adding more and more thank-you rings as we go through this book—okay?

1. Cut out rings 1, 2, and 3 from the front of this book. Start making your chain by following the easy directions on page 23.

2. Make up lots more rings of your own to add to your THANK-YOU CHAIN—all about YOU! Draw pictures on your rings or color them. Have fun!

3. Cut out the Beautiful Bible Bookmark from the inside back cover. Have someone help you find I Thessalonians 5:18. Read the verse out loud. Put the Beautiful Bible Bookmark **right there** in your very own Bible!

What a Wonderful World!

HELLO
TIME

Hello, again! Did you have fun starting your THANK-YOU CHAIN? I did. And today, we are going to make it even longer. Won't that be fun?

Do you remember our wonderful Bible verse?

VERSE
TIME

"In everything give thanks . . . "
(I Thessalonians 5:18a)

Isn't that a great verse? And it is so easy to say, isn't it?
Can you say it again by yourself?

I think it is so much fun getting to know you.

I've been wondering **where you live**.

I live in a really nice place called SPOKANE, WASHINGTON, in the U.S.A.

We have lots of nice trees to climb and lots of nice parks to play in and lots of nice people to visit.

We have birds to watch and puppies to pet and places to go!
I like it here. I like it a LOT!

THANK YOU, God, for my city!

Where do **you** live in God's big, wide, wonderful world?

Tell me **all about** the neat place YOU live.

1. _____

2. _____

3. _____

4. _____

That is a great place to live, isn't it?

THANK YOU, God, for_____!
(name of place)

I'm glad God gave **you** a nice place to live.
I'm glad God gave **me** a nice place to live.

Thank You, God . . .
for places to live!

7

In fact, I am thankful for ALL of God's **whole wide wonderful world**, aren't you?

What are some things **you** are thankful for about God's wonderful world? Fill in the blanks with some things you think of.

THANK YOU, God, for the blue, blue _____ way up so high!

THANK YOU for the green, green_____, and the red, red _____,

and for yellow, yellow _____.

THANK YOU, God, for GREAT BIG _____, and for itsy bitsy _____.

I like the warm, warm sunshine, and I like the cold, cold snow.

I like God's wind that goes WHOOOOOSH! and I like God's ocean that goes SWOOSH!

What are some **other** things YOU like about God's whole wide wonderful world?

1._____

2._____

3._____

OH, YES! I am thankful for ALL of God's wonderful world, aren't you?

8

Dear God,
THANK YOU for the nice place where I live.
THANK YOU for the whole wide wonderful world.
I like it here.
THANK YOU, THANK YOU, THANK YOU, GOD!
Amen

GOOD-BYE
TIME

Wasn't this FUN? I'll bet you will have **lots**
of extra THANK-YOU rings to add to your
beautiful THANK-YOU CHAIN today . . .
all about God's wonderful world.

I'll see you next time.

SOMETHING
FUN-TO-DO

1. Cut out rings 4, 5, and 6 from the front of this book and add to your
THANK-YOU CHAIN. Make lots of EXTRA rings for your chain . . . all about God's
beautiful world.

2. Show someone else how to make a THANK-YOU CHAIN, or let him or her add
   THANK-YOU rings to your chain. Have fun!

I Like People

HELLO TIME

Hi, there! How are you today? Did you add lots and lots of rings about God's wonderful world to your THANK-YOU CHAIN? Is your chain getting long? Mine is!

I didn't KNOW we had so many things to tell God THANK YOU for, did you?

Let's say our wonderful Bible verse out loud, okay?

VERSE TIME

"In everything give thanks . . . "
(I Thessalonians 5:18a)

What a good verse we have, and it is easy to remember. Can you say it again? Good for you!

Today we are going to talk about something very SPECIAL to me . . . people! Do you like people? I do.

God makes all kinds of people, you know.
   He makes great big grown-ups.
   He makes little tiny babies.
   And He makes medium-sized kids in between!

And God LOVES His people, because He makes them so special . . . a lot like HIMSELF! (Now, that is special!)

I have some wonderful people in **my** life, do you?
People are important, and I am very VERY THANKFUL for the people in **my** life. Here they are:

Herman is my brother. He lives on a cattle ranch and rides horses.

Uncle Carl likes to make people laugh.

Roald is my husband. I love him a lot.

Aunt Nina is a good cook.

Rondi and Leif laugh and laugh and laugh. They are my children, and we are good friends.

Rolf and DeAnn take good care of their baby girls, my grandchildren—Kjerste and Kaitlund.

These are the people in MY FAMILY! I like them. I like them a lot!
In fact, I LOVE them. I love them **so much** that I can't even tell you in words how special they are to me.
THANK YOU, THANK YOU, THANK YOU, GOD, for my SPECIAL FAMILY!
Now, I want to know all about YOUR SPECIAL FAMILY!
Tell me about the members of YOUR family RIGHT NOW!
WOW! You **do** have some special people in your family, too.
Let's say THANK YOU, THANK YOU, THANK YOU, GOD for your SPECIAL FAMILY!

11

Do you have any nice FRIENDS? I do!
Here are some of MY good friends:

Bobbin lives in Montana.

Pat writes nice stories.

Bill is my cousin and my friend.
He is FUN!

Linda and Jean and Claude and Don all go to my church.

Cathy and Julie work hard in Illinois.

Chris likes to travel. She is fun, too!

I like my friends. I like them a lot.
THANK YOU, THANK YOU, THANK YOU, GOD, FOR MY GOOD FRIENDS!

Now, tell me about some of **your** good, good friends.

Which friends do you have fun with?

Which friends come to your house to visit?

My, I like your friends, too! They sound like fun to me. Let's say THANK YOU, THANK YOU, THANK YOU, GOD for ALL these GOOD FRIENDS!

Oh, yes. I like people. People **are** important. And I think people need other people, don't you?

You see, we need people to talk with and to walk with. We need people to laugh with and to cry with.
We need people to love!
We need people who share and who care . . . **ABOUT US!**

Oh, yes, THANK YOU, God, for PEOPLE!

PRAYER TIME

THANK YOU, God, for my nice family.
THANK YOU, God, for my good friends.
I like people.
THANK YOU, THANK YOU, THANK YOU, GOD!
Amen

GOOD-BYE TIME

WOW! We can add lots of rings to our THANK-YOU CHAIN today, can't we? I'm going to put a ring on my chain for each person in my family. I might even add some for my friends. I'd better get busy.
See you next time! Good-bye!

SOMETHING FUN-TO-DO

1. Cut out rings 7, 8, and 9 from the cover of this book and add them to your THANK-YOU CHAIN.

2. Add EXTRA rings with the names (and faces) of the IMPORTANT PEOPLE in your life. Is your chain as long as a mile yet? Have fun!

Happy Times

HELLO TIME

Well, HELLO AGAIN!

It is **so good** to see you. Are you ready for another fun time? I am.

Do you like to **laugh**? Do you like to **smile**?

I DO!

Heee, heee, HEEE!   Haaa, haaa, HAAA!   Hooo, hooo, HOOO!

I like feeling HAPPY, don't you?
And when I am happy, I am thankful!

Like our nice Bible verse says:

VERSE TIME

"In everything give thanks . . . "
(I Thessalonians 5:18a)

I do!

14

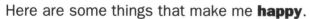

Here are some things that make me **happy**.

When somebody **tickles** me I wiggle . . .
and giggle! That makes me laugh!

THANK YOU, God, for tickles.

When I turn somersaults down a hill
I roll over and over and over
until at the bottom . . . PLOP! . . . I STOP!
That makes me laugh!

THANK YOU, God,
for somersaults.

And when our dog **jumps**, he
wags his tail . . . ALL OVER ME
. . . thump, thump, thump!
Right in my face! That makes me
LAUGH!

THANK YOU, God,
for dogs.

And when I blow on the candles
on my birthday cake . . . WHOOSH!
. . . and they ALL GO OUT!
Then I **really** smile!

THANK YOU, God,
for cakes
and candles
and birthdays!

What are some other things that make YOU laugh and smile?

1._____ 2._____ 3._____

15

But we don't always have to **laugh** or **smile** to be happy.
Sometimes being happy is just on the INSIDE . . . where we **feel**.
I feel happy when I catch a snowflake on my tongue and let it melt.

THANK YOU, God, for snowflakes.

I feel happy when I hear my kitty cat purr, purr, purrrr. That even **sounds** happy.

THANK YOU, God, for kitty cats.

I feel happy when
I watch a beautiful sunset.

THANK YOU, God,
for sunsets.

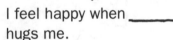

I feel happy when _____ hugs me.
I feel happy when I do something nice for someone.
And I really feel happy when I crawl into my warm, cozy bed at night, and get tucked in . . .
nice and tight . . .
good-night!
THEN I feel HAPPY!

THANK YOU, God,
for hugs and warm beds!

What are some other things that make you feel happy **inside**?

1._____ 2._____ 3._____

PRAYER TIME

Dear God,
THANK YOU for FUN!
THANK YOU for things that make me laugh and smile.
But most of all, God,
THANK YOU for **being with me** . . . ALL OF THE TIME!
That **really** makes me happy.
Amen

GOOD-BYE TIME

My, this was a fun day, wasn't it? It makes me smile
as long as a mile just to think about it.
I will see you next time!
Good-bye!

SOMETHING FUN-TO-DO

1. Cut out rings 10 and 11 and add them to your beautiful THANK-YOU CHAIN. How long is your chain getting?

2. Add MILES and MILES to your chain by making extra rings with HAPPY THINGS on them.

3. Count how many times you laugh OUT LOUD today! Have fun!

Thank You for EVERYTHING

HELLO TIME

Hi!
Do you know what? I'm getting **sad**. You see, this is the last devotion in this book, and I WILL MISS YOU!
We have had so much fun together being thankful, haven't we?

Do you remember our nice Bible verse?

VERSE TIME

"In everything give thanks . . . "
(I Thessalonians 5:18a)

You know, there are SO MANY things to tell God THANK YOU for that I can't even remember all of them, can you?

Let's see if we can remember **some** of them.

THANK YOU, God, for the special way You made ME!

THANK YOU, God, for this whole great big wide wonderful **world**!

THANK YOU for all the nice **people** in my life.

THANK YOU for things that make me **laugh** and **smile**!

There! We **did** it. We remembered a lot of things to be thankful for, didn't we? GOOD FOR US!

But . . . is that all? Did we forget anything?

Is there anything **else** we should be thankful for?

Oh, my goodness gracious me!

YES THERE IS !

There are about a **million, jillion, zillion, trillion** other things we could say THANK YOU for.

Can you think of any? _____

How about this one?

> THANK YOU, God, for my life . . . for letting me be **alive . . . right now**!
> I **like** being alive, don't you? I like it a lot!

THANK YOU, THANK YOU, THANK YOU, God . . . for my life!

Here are some more things we almost forgot.

> THANK YOU, God, for **air** to breathe,
> and **food** to eat, and **clothes** to wear.

THANK YOU, THANK YOU, THANK YOU, God!
We'd better not forget those things.

Let's see. Can you think of anything else?

Oh, yes. Here's one.

THANK YOU, God, for Your **Holy Bible** and all the **wise words** You gave us to live by. THANK YOU FOR THE BIBLE, GOD!

How about HEAVEN?
Did we thank God for HEAVEN yet? I didn't.
We'd better do that!

THANK YOU, God, for **heaven**. We know heaven is a special place. It is safe there.
THANK YOU, GOD, FOR HEAVEN!

Oh, dear. I almost forgot
the VERY MOST IMPORTANT ONE!

We can't forget to tell God THANK YOU for JESUS!

Thank You, God, for **Jesus, Your Son**!
I **like** Jesus. I **love** Jesus.
And HE loves ME! Isn't that GREAT?

THANK YOU, THANK YOU, THANK YOU, GOD, FOR JESUS!

There. Now can you think of **anything else?** What if we forget something . . . something **important**?

Oh dear, oh dear! WHAT SHALL WE DO??!

I KNOW! I have an idea. Let's tell God,

THANK YOU FOR EVERYTHING

PRAYER TIME

GOOD-BYE TIME

God, You are SO GOOD to us. You give us so much.
THANK YOU, God.
THANK YOU, THANK YOU,
THANK YOU . . . for **EVERYTHING**!
Amen

Whew! Being thankful can be hard work, can't it?
I think I am ready for a NAP! But not quite yet.
I still have to add today's rings to my
THANK-YOU CHAIN. Mine is getting
really, really, REALLY long. Is yours?

I think I will add an extra-special
ring on my chain today that
says I am thankful for YOU!

21

Thank you for going through this book with me. I had fun. I hope you did, too. Maybe we can go through **another** Fun-to-Do Devotional together sometime soon. I'd like that a lot.

But now, I have to say good-bye. I'm thankful God introduced YOU to ME.
I like having you for a special friend.

THANK YOU, THANK YOU, THANK YOU, GOD!

Good-bye from your friend,

SOMETHING FUN-TO-DO

1. Keep adding rings to your THANK-YOU CHAIN.
   See how long you can make it. Today, add rings 12, 13, and 14.

2. Save your chain to use as a decoration for a special holiday.
   Add more links to it each time you use it. Have fun!

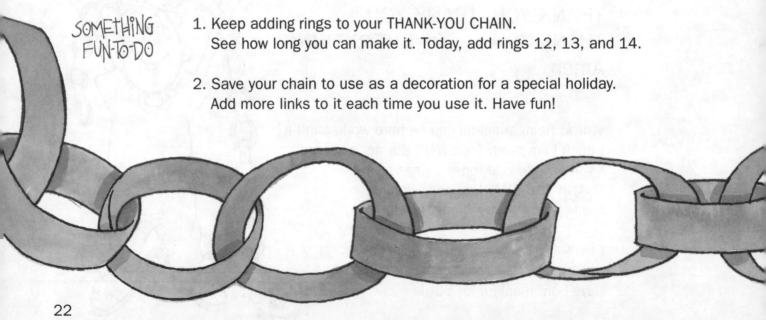

Simple, easy-to-follow instructions for
how to make **your** THANK-YOU CHAIN.

On the inside of the front and back covers, you will find some beautiful rings for our beautiful THANK-YOU CHAIN. These are just the beginning, though. We are going to have lots of fun being THANKFUL!

1. Cut out the THANK YOU rings from the inside front and back covers of this book, two or three for each devotion as listed in Something Fun to Do.

2. Tape the ends of ring 1 together to form a circle.

3. Loop each additional ring through the last ring and tape the ends together to form a chain.

4. Use one strip as a pattern and cut out lots of **extra rings** from colored paper. Encourage your child to decorate each ring with a picture (or word) of something he or she is thankful for. See how **long** a chain the child can make. (**Go ahead, make one for yourself!** But be certain that your chain isn't longer or "better" than your child's. Or you can make this into a **family project**.) Make the chain as simple or elaborate as you choose.

5. Use your chain (or chains) to decorate the kitchen, living room, child's bedroom, etc.

6. HAVE FUN with your child! (I wish I could be there, too!)

Remember: Every day is THANKSGIVING DAY! This is one chain that is truly ENDLESS!

Dear Parents,

I'm so glad you have chosen this Fun-to-Do Devotions book to do with your child and with **me**! You won't need much time to go through these fun devotions, but be sure the time is as regular as possible—maybe after a meal or after nap time.

You don't need many things to start out, just this book and the Bible and whatever the devotion suggests to make it a really fun time for you and your child.

Each devotion uses the same elements. In each one you'll find:
- HELLO TIME
- PRAYER TIME
- VERSE TIME
- GOOD-BYE TIME
- SOMETHING FUN TO DO

Because young children learn well through repetition, the same Scripture verse is used in each devotion. By the time you finish this book, your child will probably have memorized the verse.

When you finish this book, look for more Fun-to-Do Devotions at your local Christian bookstore.

I promise—these devotions will be fun for both you and your child!

God Bless!

Christine